# The Power of PosiTiff Thinking
# Change Your Beliefs And Live A Life of Abundance

By
Tiffiney L. Hall

AFFILIATE DISCLAIMER. The short, direct, non-legal version is this: Some of the links in this report may be affiliate links which means that I earn money if you choose to buy from that vendor at some point in the near future. I do not choose which products and services to promote based upon which pay me the most, I choose based upon my decision of which I would recommend to a dear friend. You will never pay more for an item by clicking through my affiliate link, and, in fact, may pay less since I negotiate special offers for my readers that are not available elsewhere.

DISCLAIMER AND/OR LEGAL NOTICES: The information presented herein represents the view of the author as of the date of publication. Because of the rate with which conditions change, the author reserves the right to alter and update his opinion based on the new conditions. The report is for informational purposes only. While every attempt has been made to verify the information provided in this report, neither the author nor his affiliates/partners assume any responsibility for errors, inaccuracies, or omissions. Any slights of people or organizations are unintentional. If advice concerning legal or related matters is needed, the services of a fully qualified professional should be sought. This report is not intended for use as a source of legal or accounting advice. You should be aware of any laws which govern business transactions or other business practices in your country and state. Any reference to any person or business whether living or dead is purely coincidental.

# The Power of PosiTiff Thinking Affirmations

***I am 100% grateful for money.***

I am generous, big-hearted, and ready to help anyone in need. Wealth naturally flows to me, and as a result, I am grateful. I am grateful for abundant graces and generosity.

***I refuse to let past beliefs keep me from getting the wealth that I deserve.***

I reject any myths that I have believed that are unsupportive of my goals. I embrace my natural greatness and attract good things.

***I make more than enough money.***

When I make any money, I am filled with gratitude. I say, "Thank you," for even the smallest amounts of money, because gratitude fills me with joy and attracts more good things into my life.

***My Focus Is On Abundance.***

What I focus on expands. What I give my attention to grows. My mind controls the outcomes that I experience in my life.

***I have a mindset of abundance.***

I attract positive things because I constantly think about positive things. My outer life is extremely positive because my inner life is also extremely positive.

***Because I focus on good things, I attract good things into my life.***

I attract wealth, goodness, and beauty. I gratefully receive the abundance that is provided to me.

***I Am choosing to manifest my dreams.***

Today, I choose to take massive action on my dreams. I know that when I combine my abundance mindset with massive action, I truly achieve limitless results. I avoid waiting for things to happen. I make them happen.

***I Am achieving my biggest dreams.***

Nothing can stop me. I am relentless in pursuing them. This belief gives me great confidence as I pursue my dreams.

***I attract abundance. When I combine abundance with action, my dreams will come true...***

I am excited to see all the good things happening in my life. I keep pushing and striving until I reach the success that I desire, and my dreams come true.

# TABLE OF CONTENTS

INTRODUCTION

# Live A Life Of Abundance

What would you say if I told you that you could have more? Having more isn't so much about changing the way you work as much as it is changing the way you think? And what if I told you that you have the ability to make as much as you want?

Would you think I was crazy?

I can certainly understand that. After all, for our entire lives, we've been told that the only way to have more is to work harder or get rich by winning the lottery.

The odds of you winning the lottery are slim to non– and there's a much easier way to have more.

And while there's certainly some truth to it, if you work hard, you can have more, but you can definitely still have more without working harder.

There's no direct correlation between how hard you work and how much you have.

Think about it as if you work for a salary. You can work incredibly hard and only get a 3% raise.

No matter how hard you work…

...you're still limited by your salary.

However, there is a direct correlation between your mindset and how much more you can have.

In other words, the way you think about abundance has a real and direct influence on how much more you can actually have.

Your mindset can either:

Catapult you to live a life of abundance or

keep you stuck living in lack, scarcity, struggle, and despair.

That's The Power of PosiTiff Thinking.

This is why most people never reach the levels of success they truly desire. They don't have an effective mindset about how to achieve that level of success. They're trapped where they are and don't know how to change.

They've done things a particular way for so long that they can't see any other way.

In his book Secrets Of The Millionaire Mind, T. Harv Ecker says:

> "The reality is that most people do not reach their full potential. Most people are not successful. Research shows that 80 percent of individuals will never be financially free in the way they'd like to be, and 80 percent will never claim to be truly happy. The reason is simple. Most people are unconscious. They are a little asleep at the wheel. They work and think on a superficial level of life—based only on what they can see. They live strictly in the visible world."

Does this describe you?

- Not financially free?

- Not reaching your full potential?
- Not truly happy?
- Feeling like you're stuck in a valley?

You know that you should be living a life of abundance, but you just can't quite seem to get there.

Then this book is for you.

This book will challenge many of the beliefs that you've had for years and help restructure your thinking.

The only prerequisite is having an open mind.

Some of what you're about to read may contradict beliefs you've held about for years. Beliefs that have been passed down from one generation to the next in your family, in your community, in your place of worship, and even amongst your peers. Unfortunately, these beliefs have been holding you back from living a life of abundance.

It's time for you to change those beliefs and embrace living the abundant life you deserve.

It's time to stop being – stuck in the valley- and make the climb to the mountaintop of abundance.

Ready? Let's Climb!

# Change Your Money Beliefs

There's a good chance that what you believe about money is simply wrong. You've been conditioned by our parents, in our communities, and by your peers to believe certain things about money.

And most of us have believed those things without EVER questioning them.

Again, to quote T. Harv Ecker:

> "You were taught how to think and act when it comes to money. These teachings become your conditioning, which becomes automatic responses that run you for the rest of your life. Unless, of course, you intercede and revise your mind's money files."

As a result of these beliefs, you have what I'd like to call a "toxic" relationship with money:

- You want more of it and can never seem to get enough of it.

You know that money can achieve good things but feel conflicted having it.

- You're grateful when we have money to purchase the things we want, but also feel like we're being selfish.

You were taught how to think, feel, and act when it comes to money. In turn you become your conditioned, which creates an automatic response that you have for the rest of your life. Unless, of course, you break the ties that bind you to those beliefs.

Why do we have this "toxic" relationship with money? Why do we get so tied up in knots over it? Why do we stress about it so much? Why can't we just leave this "toxic" relationship in the past?

It's because a lot of what you've believed a lot of about money just isn't true.

And we've never questioned our beliefs to determine if they're actually true. And because we've never questioned them, we haven't achieved the levels of success that we truly desire.

In her book You Are A Badass At Making Money, Jen Sincero says:

> "Our beliefs, along with our thoughts and words, are at the root of everything we experience in life, which is why consciously choosing what rolls around in your mind and falls out of your mouth is one of the most important things you can do. This conscious choosing of your thoughts, beliefs, and words is called mastering your mindset, and master it you must if you'd like to live large and in charge."

If you want more success, money, and happiness, then it's crucial that you change your beliefs about money myths and adapt The Power of PosiTiff Thinking and master your money mindset.

Mastering your money mindset requires taking a close look at what you've believed for so long and determining if there is any real truth to it.

Let's look at some of the common money beliefs.

BELIEF #1

## Money Is Evil

"Money is the root of all evil." At some point in our lives, we've all heard this. Maybe your parents reinforced this myth when you were growing up. They didn't want to have too much money because they were afraid that it would result in evil.

And so, you've unconsciously been conditioned to take on this same belief.

- You don't want to accumulate too much money because you're afraid of what it will do to you.
- You believe that somehow money will turn you evil.
- Or you believe that money itself is evil.

Is money really evil? Is there any truth to that?

No.

Take a minute and think about what money actually is.

Money is printed paper. Or a hunk of metal, like a gold bar. Or some digital numbers in your bank account that fluctuate up and down.

Is that paper or metal inherently evil?

Nope.

Money itself has neutral power. It's not good and it's not bad.

Think about it this way. When you put a $20 bill in your wallet, does that suddenly make you and evil person?

No, it definitely doesn't.

But what if you put a $100 bill in your wallet?

Guess what you're still not an evil person.

That's because money itself is not evil.

Adding more money to your bank account doesn't mean that you're doing something evil or bad. It's simply fluctuating your account in a positive direction.

It's not money itself that's good or bad, it's what you do with money, that is either good or bad.

- You can give it to people in need.
- You can start a charity.
- You can help your friend start a business.

And, of course, you can also do bad things with money. We won't share ideals to encourage that.

I think you get the point. It's the actions you take, not money itself, that's evil.

So, let's change this belief. Money has neutral power, it's not evil.

BELIEF #2

## People Who Want Money Are Greedy

There is the assumption that only people who want money are greedy. They assumption that if we want money, we'll become like Ebenezer Scrooge, just hoarding money.

But is this true?

Again, money has neutral power. It's what you do with money that truly matters.

So yes, you can be greedy and want to accumulate as much money as possible and hoard it.

But having more money also allows you to be extremely generous. It allows you to give good things to others. It allows you to donate to charity.

You simply can't do those things if you don't have money.

You can't be generous if you don't have money.

Think about that.

If you want to be financially generous, you have to have some finances in the first place.

It's time to change this belief. Wanting more money does not make you greedy.

BELIEF #3

## There Is Not Enough Money

If you grew up in a house where finances were regularly "tight" or everyone was always "broke", you may believe that there is not enough money.

You were conditioned to believe the reason you don't have enough money is because there simply isn't enough money to go around. Remember, money doesn't grow on trees!

But let's think about the truth of this and evaluate this belief.

How much money is in the world?

Trillions and trillions of dollars.

There is more than enough money for everyone. There is not a scarcity of money.

In fact, there is an actual abundance of money in the world.

Just because you don't have all the money that you want doesn't mean that there's not enough money. This is the difference between a "scarcity" mindset and an "abundance" mindset:

- A scarcity mindset believes there is never enough. You feel like you have to hold onto everything you have because you never know when it will be gone.
- An abundance mindset believes there is more than enough for everyone. When you get money, it doesn't mean that someone lacks money.

So, as you see, money is not an end all to be all. In other words, you having more money does not mean that someone else is losing money.

There is more than enough money in the world for everyone to have as much as they want.

Let's change this belief. There's more than enough for everyone. We live in a world of abundance.

BELIEF #4

## I'll Never Make Enough Money

If you believe that you will never make enough money, then you will certainly never make enough money.

Again, you were conditioned to believe this.

If there is more than enough money in the world for everyone, why would you believe that you'll never make enough?

You're have incredible talents and so much to offer the world, and it's important that you believe that. Your skills, talents, and expertise are worth money, and there are lots of people out there who are willing to pay for those skills.

But in order for this to become your reality, you have to first change this belief.

You have to stop believing that you'll never make enough money and start affirming that you are going to make more money than you can imagine.

At this very moment, you may not know exactly how you're going to make the money, but that's okay.

You have to master your mindset, which means having the unshakeable belief that you're going to abundantly increase your income.

Let's change this belief. You can and will make more than enough money if you're willing to first affirm it and believe it.

BELIEF #5

## If I Make More Money, People Won’t Like Me

If your parent didn’t like people who had money, you were probably conditioned to have this same belief.

Do people really dislike people who have money? We dislike people who flaunt their wealth in an arrogant way.

There again, this goes back to how people use money.

If you make more money and then start bragging to your friends about how awesome you are, then they may not like you anymore.

But if you use your wealth to help others, people will actually like you more! And they certainly won’t dislike you for spending some on yourself.

Let’s change this belief. As long as you don’t flaunt your wealth in an annoying, arrogant way, people will continue to like you. In fact, people will probably appreciate you more as you accumulate more wealth.

BELIEF #6

## I'm Just Fine Without Money

If you've struggled for a long time to achieve financial stability, then you may have convinced yourself that you're just fine without money.

But is this really true?

- Are you really living your absolute best life?
- Are you the best version of yourself?
- Are you living a life of abundance?

Let's be honest: money makes many things possible that aren't possible.

Money allows you to expand your horizons.

If you don't have money, you can't expand and you can't be your best self.

I'm not saying that people without money are defective. I am saying that money gives you the ability to be effective in how you live.

Let's change this belief. You are just fine with money, it's necessary to make it possible to live the way you want to live.

# Thoughts Are Powerful, Think Abundance

Your mind and what you think is incredibly powerful . Far more powerful than you can even imagine.

What you think and how you think has an incredible effect on your quality of life and what you manifest. Your mind controls most of your reality:

- What you think about…
- What you give your attention to…
- What you focus on...

...literally controls the outcomes in your life.

Marcus Aurelius said:

> "The happiness of your life depends upon the quality of your thoughts. Therefore, guard accordingly, and take care that you entertain no notions unsuitable to virtue and reasonable nature."

This is so true. To live a life of abundance depends primarily upon your thoughts. That's how powerful your mind works. That's how powerful your thoughts are.

If you want to live a life of abundance and attract more, it's necessary to adopt a positive mindset.

You must think abundance.

Because of this, it's absolutely essential that we learn to master the way we think about abundance and wealth.

## Your Thoughts Control Your Outcomes

What most people fail to realize is the outcome of your reality begins with your thoughts. Every outcome you experience, whether positive or negative, is primarily the result of your thoughts.

Or, to put it another way, what you think, you are. What you think you become.

What you think about, what you focus determines what you attract into your life:

- Focus on positive things and you'll attract positive things.
- Focus on negative things and you'll attract negative things.

Yes, your thoughts are really that powerful.

Again, as Jen Sincero says:

> "...we can literally create the reality we desire by making ourselves think and believe what we desire to think and believe."

Or as T. Harv Ecker puts it:

> "Whatever results you're getting, be they rich or poor, good, or bad, positive or negative, always remember that your outer world is simply a reflection of your inner world. If things aren't going well in your outer life, it's because things aren't going well in your inner life. It's that simple."

Can you clearly see where this is going? As Ecker says, your outer world (reality) is simply a reflection of your inner world (your thoughts, desires, and dreams).

If you're not experiencing what you want in your life, it's primarily due to what's happening in your inner world.

- Not attracting the wealth, you want? Inner world.
- Not able to get your head above water financially? Inner world.
- Not able to move forward in your job like you should? Inner world.

No one but you can control your inner world.

You determine what you think about and focus on. The more you master control over your inner world, the more you will control and shape your reality (outer world).

That may seem like a a lot to think about, but it's amazing to know. It's something that you and only you can control.

So, what it means, if you want to change your life and live a life of abundance, you absolutely must master the way you think.

## Mind On Your Money, Money On Your Mind

If your outer world is a reflection of your inner world, then it's absolutely necessary that you master how you think about money. You need to change your beliefs from what you were conditioned to believe in the past and adopt an abundance mindset.

If you have a scarcity mindset, believing that there is never enough money, then that is exactly what you will attract into your life. You will attract scarcity. You attract exactly what you focus on.

But if you believe in the abundance of the world, and that you can live a life of abundance, you'll attract abundance into your life. If you believe that there is more than enough for you and everyone else, you'll begin manifesting that in your life.

What you believe becomes your reality.

Therefore, it's important to believe:

- There's enough money for everyone.
- You simply need to do the work to get it.

Think about all the abundance in the world. You simply need to open yourself up to receive it.

Whether you believe in a high power greater than yourself or not, you need to master that there is energy behind all things, you must believe that higher wants you to live a life of abundance. Because where thoughts flow, energy goes.

The world is full of abundance, and if you're living in scarcity, then you're not living a life of abundance and all that the world has to offer.

It's time to not only change your beliefs about money, but also change the way you think about money. To believe that there's enough, that you deserve to have money, and that you were created to experience and live a life of abundance.

Regularly affirm this, go back, and read the affirmations in the beginning of the book. Talk to yourself about these things over and over again until they're etched into your brain. Until you believe them with all your heart, soul, and at the core of your very being.

## The Universe is Full of Opportunities

Once you begin embracing an abundance mindset, you open yourself up to more, and you'll start seeing opportunities everywhere.

- You'll see ways to acquire more of things that you never seen before.
- Opportunities will come out of nowhere.
- You'll begin to attract more money than you could ever imagine.

But you must open your mind to what's impossible becoming possible all around you. The world is full of infinite opportunities, and just because you can't see them at this very moment doesn't mean they're not there.

Angelina Zimmerman put it this way:

> "The scarcity pathway leads one to experience a life not fully lived, a life that can only be described as pedestrian. Overflowing with strong negative reactions like the high tide that creates waves in a rock pool not to mention the countless missed opportunities and experiences.
>
> Those who choose to walk the path of abundance experience a completely different life. Opting to live life to the full, exuding happiness, generous by nature, creative and inspirational. Taking full advantage and enjoying the

wave of opportunities that come their way, along with memorable experiences."

Today, choose abundance.

One of the best ways to choose abundance is through the practice of gratitude.

Start practicing gratitude for all the things your currently have in your life. When you receive, a simple, "thank you" will suffice. Trust me, such a small practice will start to transform your life.

When you're grateful for even the smallest things, you send out positive energy out into the universe that attracts more positive things into your life.

It's powerful. You put out the positive energy of gratitude and you are rewarded with more things to be grateful for.

Begin practicing gratitude immediately, like right now simply say "thank you." As you shift your mindset from scarcity to abundance, you'll be amazed by all the good things that will begin to come into your life.

# Take Action To Manifest Your Dreams

An abundance mindset is absolutely, positively necessary if you want to manifest your dreams.

But having an abundance mindset by itself is not enough.

You must take ACTION.

You must begin taking action on making your dreams reality.

When you have an abundance mindset, and you begin to take action on your dreams…

...you truly have the ability to achieve the impossible.

There is absolutely nothing that can stop you. You will achieve more than you ever thought possible.

In other words, you may have an abundance mindset, but if you don't begin to take action on your dreams, nothing will change. However, an abundance mindset partnered with action will lead to the mountaintop of greatness.

The equation is:

Abundance + Action = Manifestation

Once you begin taking action, you'll see the things you dreamed about manifest in reality.

Isn't that something to think about? Doesn't that give you a new found energy?

When taking action to manifest your dreams, take the follow steps…

STEP # 1

## Write It Down, Make It Real

The first step is to write down your dreams on paper. Be intentional and specific when you're writing. You want to be so intention and specific that you can see yourself doing it, as if it's real.

Ask yourself questions like:

- What are my biggest dreams?
- What do I want to get out of life?
- What do I want to accomplish?
- How much money do I want to make?
- When do I want to make it by?

The more intentional and specific you can be when writing down your dreams, the more you'll be able to visualize them coming true.

The more you can visualize them, the more positive emotion you'll feel around them and the more focused you'll be on them.

And the more focused you are on your dreams, the more you'll attract them into your life.

It's really that simple.

T. Harv Ecker calls this the wealth principle:

**WEALTH PRINCIPLE:**

"Thoughts lead to feelings. Feelings lead to actions. Actions lead to results."

So, write down your dreams and goals with as many details as possible. Feel them like it's already happening. Imagine the feeling you'll have when you accomplish them.

It's those thoughts and feelings that will lead to actions, which will then transform into the most amazing results.

After you've written down your dreams, Recite, Rehearse, Repeat them again and again. Practice what I call the 3R formula every single day. This affirms that they are going to come true.

Say things like:

- "I affirm that I am going to double my income by (a specific) date."
- "I affirm that I am financial abundant in all areas of my life."

3Rs and affirmations will have you believe with all your heart your dreams will manifest in reality.

Raise your energy level and feelings around these affirmations until you're ready to move and take actions on them, unapologetically.

Even if you don't know how these things are going to happen, affirm them as though they will. These affirmations create positive energy around you that will keep you motivated and on focus.

As Gary John Bishop says:

> "...the person who views success as if it were just around the corner will not only work his butt off to achieve it but be energized and alive to it all the while acting on that fundamental view [abundance] of success....You see, our thoughts are so powerful that they are constantly pushing you toward your goals, even when you don't realize what those goals actually are! Your brain is wired to win."

And remember, the energy you give out to the world is the same energy that comes back to you.

If you put out positive energy in the form of affirmations and gratitude, you'll see that positive energy coming back to you in positive ways.

STEP #2

## Make A Plan, Make It Plain

Once you've written them down to make them real, and recite, rehearse, repeat, it's necessary to create movement to manifest your dreams.

Make a plan and make it plain. Map out what specific steps you need to follow in order to achieve your dreams, and then begin taking those actions.

What do you need to do in order to make your dreams a reality? Don't worry if you don't have it all figured out at this very. Just begin to make a plan to take action on whatever comes to mind.

- Do you need to ask someone?
- Hire a mentor?
- Start a business?
- Send an email to an important contact?

If you have an abundance mindset and are open to new opportunities, actions will begin to pop into your mind. You'll start to have ideas that you never had before.

Take action on these ideas. These will be cues that guide you on the path to how to get there.

Make a plan to take some sort of action, whether big or small, towards manifesting your dreams every single day. Each and every day, move a little bit closer to achieving what you truly desire in life.

When something comes to your mind, write it down, make it a part of the plan, and take action.

The more you take action, the more you will see the results manifest. You'll realize that you truly do have the ability to achieve the impossible. You'll achieve things you never imagined or believed were possible.

## Your Dreams Are Waiting for You

And now for the BIG question: what are you going to do?

You now know:

- You truly have limitless potential.
- Most of the myths you've believed about money are totally false.
- Your inner thoughts control your outer reality.
- You have the power to shape your reality.
- You can attract and manifest the wealth and dreams that you desire.
- The Creator totally has your back and is supporting your dreams.

Are you going to start taking action on your dreams? Or are you going to continue to sit in the valley, staring at the mountaintop?

Are you ready to take control of your reality, change your money beliefs, and achieve your dreams or continue to do nothing?

There is an amazing future out there, waiting for you to take advantage of every opportunity before you. Don't let anything control your future but you. Don't look back at your life 30 years from now and regret opportunities that you didn't take.

There is no better day than today. Remember, change your money beliefs, thoughts are powerful, think positive, and take actions to manifest your dreams through The Power of PosiTiff Thinking Change Your Beliefs And Live A Life Of Abundance.

Now, you are ready to make the climb to the mountaintop of abundance, let's go!

# Reflection Questions

**What is your reaction when you hear that making money is just as much about your mindset as it is about your actions?**

**What comes to mind when you think about what it takes to accumulate wealth?**

**Are you achieving the level of success that you want? What thoughts or beliefs are holding you back?**

**What conditioned beliefs do you have about money?**

**On a scale of "terrible" to "great", how would you rate your "toxic" relationship with money?**

**What beliefs about money have you never questioned? Why have you believed this?**

**Do you see money as evil? Does your belief align with the reality about money?**

**What do you believe about those who want more money? Are your beliefs correct?**

**Do you have a scarcity or abundance mindset when it comes to money? How can you tell?**

**What are some of the good things that you could accomplish if you had more money?**

**Do you tend to focus most of your attention on positive or negative things?**

**Does your mindset attract the wealth and success that you desire?**

**How much are you in control of your "inner world" (thoughts, desires, and dreams)? How can you strengthen your control?**

**Why is a scarcity mindset unhelpful when it comes to achieving success?**

**What are some simple ways you can immediately begin practicing gratitude?**

**Why is taking action so critically important?**

**What dreams do you want to achieve? Do you believe that you can achieve them? How?**

**What is the "wealth principle" and how does it lead to massive success?**

**What affirmations will you repeat every single day?**

**What specific steps will you take toward making your dreams come true? What action can you take today?**

## Thank You's & Dedications

First, foremost, and always, I thank God for His grace and mercy. I never imagined I would be sharing my thoughts and ideals at this level. When I finally surrendered, I discovered that His plan for my life has been bigger than I imagined.

I dedicate this book to my grandfather, grandmother, and uncle. Thank you for a family legacy built on love

My backbone, my love, my husband Jahmal "Jay." I wasn't this person when we got married and you have been so supportive in who I have become. I thank for telling me you saw in me something I didn't see in myself, a much-needed safe space for people. I'll never forget "people like you."

My children James and Jaylin, look at your mother now. I am a better human being looking at the two of you and seeing something that I did right in this world. Both of you were "easy" to raise and know, even in those moments when we struggled, on Hale, we struggled together, and I've had fun watching you both grow from the very beginning.

My mother, there would be no me without you. No matter what it may have felt like at times, I always felt your love and know that you are proud of your one and only, magnificent daughter!

My sister-cousins thank you for being my first best friends and always a source of encouragement.

My aunts, cousins, extended family, and friends, thank you for the love and support.

To Tajuanna, you saw me when I was most vulnerable. This journey has been everything we prayed it would be and there is so much more to come. You are the best VA, sister-friend, prayer partner a girl could have. I love you.

To my sisters who prayed for and with me. You manifested PosiTiff, without even knowing it, Felicia, Latanya, Jacqueline. I love you.

To my sister Pat. You always showing up for me without question. Supporting me, cheering loudly, proudly, and unapologetically. I love you sis.

**Contact information for Tiffiney**

**Email: info@tiffineylhall.com**

**www.tiffineylhall.com**

9 798218 176457

Printed by Libri Plureos GmbH in Hamburg, Germany